GOD AS FATHER
In the Message of
Blessed Josemaria Escriva

GOD AS FATHER
In the Message of
Blessed Josemaria Escriva

Fernando Ocariz

Scepter Publishers
Princeton, NJ

Translated from *Vivir como Hijos de Dios, Estudios sobre el Beato Josemaria Escrivá*, © EUNSA, Pamplona, Spain, 1993
ISBN 0-933932-75-8

With ecclesiastical approval.

Cover: Detail of a copy of "The Coronation of the Virgin" by Velazquez, Lockwood Oratory, Arnold Hall Conference Center, North Pembroke, Massachusetts.

First printing, 1995
Second printing, 1997
Third printing, 1999
Fourth printing, 1999

Translation © 1994 Scepter Publishers, Inc.
Printed in the United States of America

Contents

Being a Child of God	12
Being Christ Himself	17
Through the Holy Spirit	20
Children of Mary and Joseph	23
Children of the Church and the Pope	26
Brothers and Sisters to All	27
Filial and Fraternal Spirit	29
A Child of God Everywhere	30
The Freedom of God's Children	31
Working as God's Children	34
The Prayer of God's Children	37
The Apostolate of God's Children	41
Joy, Sorrow and Death for God's Children	44
The Conversion of God's Children	48
Conclusion: the Father's little Children	51
Notes	53

SINCE HIS DEATH on June 26, 1975, countless people the world over have testified to the benefits they attribute to Blessed Josemaria Escriva. Among them are those who prize Escriva's contributions to theological development. This, despite the fact that Opus Dei's founder wrote no treatises. Rather his was a pastoral activity that led him largely to preach and to pen letters and instructions, mostly for members.

Directing himself to varying audiences, Msgr. Escriva combines depth and lucidity. Throughout, his thoughts are knit together by a careful, loving knowledge of the word of God. Alvaro del Portillo, his successor at the head of Opus Dei, can orient us in the study of his work: "Note, for example, how the author comments on the Gospel. He equally skirts mere erudition and trite convention. Each verse is thoroughly meditated and, thanks to that contemplation, yields new lights, hidden perhaps for centuries."[1]

Without doubt one of these *new lights* is a heightened awareness of divine filiation. He views it, not as one theoretical truth among many, but as the very foundation for all Christian living — a reality that can never be contemplated or echoed enough. Escriva calls this teaching "as old as the Gospel and like the Gospel new." We see it reflected in *The Way*: "'Father,' said that big lad, a good student at the university (I wonder what has become of him?), 'I was thinking about what you told me ... that I'm a son of God! and I found myself walking along the street, head up and chin out, with a feeling of pride within me ... a son of God!' With a clear conscience I advised him to foster that 'pride.'"[2]

We are God's children: more than a theological conclusion, God showed this new light to Blessed Josemaria in the midst of contemplation. He writes: "For reasons I need not go into now (but which Jesus, from the tabernacle, knows full well), life has led me to realize in a special way that I am God's son. Joyfully I have entered my Father's heart, there to rectify, to purify myself, to serve him, to understand others and find excuses for them, on the strength of his love and my own lowliness. That's why I insist now that you and I are to be made anew, to awake from the facile slumber of feebleness and to realize once more, more profoundly and keenly, our condition as God's children.

"Jesus' example, every detail of his life in those Eastern lands, invites us to penetrate this truth. 'If we admit the testimony of men,' we read, 'the testimony of God is greater' (1 Jn 5:9). And what does God's testimony consist of? Again St. John tells us: 'See what love the Father has given us, that we should be called children of God; and so we are.... Beloved, we are God's children now' (1 Jn 3:1-2)."[3]

Living as God's child also affected how Josemaria Escriva spoke of God. In his teaching "central and constant is recognition of our divine filiation. The author is ever echoing St. Paul (Rom 8: 14-17): 'For all who are led by the Spirit of God are sons of God. For you did not receive the spirit of slavery to fall back into fear, but you have received the spirit of sonship. When we cry, "Abba! Father!" it is the Spirit himself bearing witness with our spirit that we are children of God, and if children, then heirs, heirs of God and fellow heirs of Christ, provided we suffer with him in order that we may also be glorified with him.'

"The text speaks about the blessed Trinity, another leitmotif of his homilies. It also reminds us that Jesus is the way leading to the Father through the Holy Spirit. He is our brother, friend — *the* Friend — master, lord and king. Christian life, then, means keeping Christ present amid ordinary life, without abandoning our rightful place."[4]

Christian existence thus has a radical dimension, qualifying it on all fronts: living as God's children. "Divine filiation is a joyful truth, a consoling mystery. It fills our spiritual life, showing us how to speak to God, how to know and love our heavenly Father. It makes our interior struggle overflow with hope and gives us the trusting simplicity of little children. Moreover, since we're God's children, we can contemplate, in love and wonder, everything as coming from the hands of our Father, God the creator. And so we become contemplatives in the midst of the world, loving the world."[5]

Indeed, affirms Alvaro del Portillo, "this is the core idea of Blessed Escriva's message: that holiness — the fullness of Christian life — is within everybody's grasp, regardless of state or condition. Thus in all its facets ordinary life provides an opportunity for unlimited, loving dedication to God and to be an active apostle in every environment."[6] The Work God entrusted to the founder (Opus Dei) can be summed up as "a way of sanctification in daily work and in the fulfillment of a Christian's ordinary duties,"[7] that is, in the midst of the world. But in any circumstance, "holiness, as much for the priest as for lay people," Escriva wrote in 1945, "is nothing more than the perfection of Christian life, fullness of divine filiation."[8]

No wonder, then, that from the outset the founder affirmed that "divine filiation is the basis of Opus Dei's spirit."[9] It's a foundation that, being equivalent to Christian life itself in all its richness, confers on its spirit a universality, whereby thousands of persons of every background can find, and in fact have found, a way for them to travel.

Consequently this spirit, while primarily cultivated in interior life, impregnates the very apostolates Opus Dei carries out as a body. In a press interview the founder points to "the primacy we give in the organization of our apostolate to the person, to the action of the Spirit upon souls, to the dignity and freedom which derive from the divine filiation of Christians."[10]

The following pages offer a preliminary attempt at analyzing and collating the truly impressive theological richness the founder's teachings contain on divine filiation. Such a task is both easy and difficult. Easy because the texts, while profound, possess an extraordinary clarity and spiritual keenness; it's not necessary to *interpret* them and even less to dissect them, perhaps thereby draining them of life. Difficult, on the other hand, because in fact divine filiation pervades everything in both his spirit and his writings, not being limited to just some passages, however numerous. Thus, one can't merely study pages where *divine filiation* or its equivalents and derivatives appear. If Escriva speaks or writes on faith, he deals with the faith of God's children; so too with fortitude or conversion and penance, he calls for courage or conversion of *God's children*. In his life, speech and writings, every virtue, every aspect of Christian existence, and even human existence itself, is stamped with the seal of divine filiation. Hence all this teaching by itself (and even more so when gleaned from contemplation rather than simple speculation) escapes any rationalistic systematization.

This is neither the place nor time to write a spiritual biography of Escriva. That task will certainly require more than the simple objective theological analysis that concerns us here. Yet his exceptional love for God is easily read between the lines. In any case, to prepare ourselves to contemplate the mystery of divine filiation under Escriva's wing, let's turn to an episode in his life.

Escriva as a child learned to turn to God with the trust of one backed by a loving and all-powerful Father. But it was in Madrid in 1931, while on a streetcar, that God indelibly and more loftily engraved in his soul a consciousness, practically an instinct, of divine filiation. Barely three years had gone by since God entrusted him with founding Opus Dei; a universal work of such far-reaching scope and novelty that hardships and misunderstandings seemed bent on stopping it in its tracks.

Many years later he commented: "When back in 1931 God allowed those blows, I was engulfed in darkness. Yet soon, amid overwhelming bitterness, there came those words: 'You are my son' (Ps 2:7), you are Christ. I could only repeat: Abba, Father! Abba, Father! Abba! Abba! Abba! And now I see with a new light, as a new discovery, as with passing years one sees the divine hand, the wisdom of the all-powerful. You did it, Lord, so I might understand that to have the cross is to find happiness, joy. I see ever more clearly the reason: to grasp the cross is to be identified with Christ, to be Christ and God's very child."

The following pages are essentially a commentary (largely from Escriva's writings) on this compact, rich text, which is not only ascetical and mystical but theological and dogmatic as well. And one also can't help seeing God's gift to a soul singularly privileged and most faithful in corresponding to love.

Being a Child of God

God's Intent: If we look for a deep, radical and realistic understanding of our life, before all else we must raise our gaze to heaven, because only in God's global design do we encounter the why of existence. Not only are we creatures, but also "we've been put here on earth for a further purpose: to enter into communion with God himself."[11]

Human nature possesses its own consistency and dignity. Yet the ultimate reason for its creation lies beyond itself. God has created us so he could gratuitously endow us with a strictly supernatural dignity: to be his children, to reach the bliss of being *domestici Dei* (Eph 2:19): members of God's household. "We don't exist to pursue just any happiness. We have been called to penetrate the intimacy of God's own life, to know and love God the Father, God the Son and God the Holy Spirit, and to love also, with the same love of our triune God, the angels and all men. This is the great boldness of Christian faith: to attain the dignity of God's children thanks to grace raising us to a supernatural level. An incredible boldness it would be, were it not founded on the promise of salvation given us by God the Father, confirmed by Christ's blood, and reaffirmed and made possible by the Holy Spirit's constant action."[12]

Created to "attain the dignity of God's children ... to penetrate the intimacy of God": here we have the direct link between God's revealed design for humanity with the supreme mystery of the most holy Trinity. In his infinite goodness God has created all things, among them, some spiritual beings welcomed to the intimacy of his own family (the life of Father, Son and Holy Spirit) without destroying or distorting the nature proper to creatures. Divine filiation is the way this introduction, this adoption is wrought; we enter into communion with God by way of filiation, which is none other than the only-begotten Son of the Father.

We know that at history's dawn "Adam did not want to be a good child of God; he rebelled. But we also hear the echoes of that *felix culpa*: 'O happy fault,' which the whole Church will joyfully intone at the Easter vigil. God the Father, in the fullness of time, sent to the world his only-begotten Son to re-establish peace; so that by redeeming humankind from sin, 'we might receive adoption as sons' (Gal 4:5), freed from the yoke of sin, capable of partaking of the Trinity's intimacy. And so it has become possible for this new man, this new engrafting of God's children (cf. Rom 6:4-5), to free all creation from disorder, restoring all things in Christ (cf. Eph 1:5-10), who has reconciled them to God (cf. Col 1:20)."[13]

Here is real history: thanks to the divine initiative, our being God's children is either made effective and actual through grace or is discarded through sin, abandoning the Father's house.[14] Renouncing divine intimacy tragically denatures us, because to be God's child involves grace-wrought cleansing and elevating of human nature, making us "partakers of the divine nature" (2 Pet 1:4).

From the universal disorder born of original sin, we can only be regenerated (again made apt for participating in the Trinity's intimacy) by being grafted onto Christ, who "has raised us to his level, the level of God's children, by coming down to our level, the level of the children of men."[15]

Participants in divine life: Filiation is the precise way God makes us members of his family.[16] Divine familiarity is not a moral question, simply a way of behaving; rather it's founded on a real transformation, elevation, adoption. "Faith teaches that man, in the state of grace, is filled with God."[17] We are truly immersed in God, ushered into partaking of the divine life, consisting of the eternal processions of the blessed Trinity. There we have the essence and radical newness of the new creation, of the supernatural order.

To know and somehow to experience the reality of our becoming godlike emphasizes its character as gratuitous gift built on our weakness. To be members of God's family is no victory of ours, no human achievement. "Along with humility, the realization of man's great dignity and of his adoption by God weaves a single attitude. It's not our own efforts or strength that save and give us life, it's God's grace. This truth can never be forgotten. If it were, the godliness of our life would be perverted, degenerating into presumption, pride. And this would lead, sooner or later, to a breakdown of spiritual life, when the soul comes face to face with its own weakness and wretchedness."[18] Therefore, "Even when we clearly see our limitations, we can and should look at God the Father, God the Son and God the Holy Spirit and realize that we share in God's own life."[19]

This participation possesses the eternal dynamism of the intra-Trinitarian divine processions, accomplishing the supernatural marvel of "the action of the one Spirit himself, who by making us Christ's brethren leads us towards God the Father."[20] This is the ineffable marvel of divine filiation, which manifests itself as our way of "sharing in the current of love that is the mystery of God one in three."[21] This is the substance of the supernatural order: the Trinitarian mystery projected onto us or, better still, our adoption, or introduction, to live in God, through filiation, through the Son. "We have been made God's children. With this free divine decision," wrote Escriva, "the natural dignity of man has been elevated incomparably. Just as sin destroyed this marvel, the redemption remade it in an even more admirable way, leading us to participate even more strictly in the divine sonship of the Word."

Not only are we called God's children, but such we are. Not only does God, in a shower of goodness, want us to deal with him as a father. But also, in an incomparably greater display of love, he has adopted us as children in a strict though limited sense. We thus participate in the one divine sonship in the strict sense: in what constitutes the second Person of the most blessed Trinity, the only-begotten Son of the Father. "'See what love the Father has given us; that we should be called children of God; and so we are' (1 Jn 3:1). God's children, brothers of the Word made flesh, of him of whom it was said: 'In him was life, and the life was the light of men' (Jn 1:4). Children of the light, brethren of the light: such we are."[22] Brothers and sisters of the Word made flesh, of Christ our Lord — not just because he has wanted to participate in our humanity, but above all because, by God's ineffable gift, we have been made participants in his sonship, in his very self.

Reason cannot take us to these heights, because "we walk by faith, not by sight" (2 Cor 5:7). Theology as it turns mystical must be theological life, contemplation. In its explanations illuminated by faith and contemplation, the way of analogy with the natural order can always help us.

To participate in the sonship of the Only-begotten, the very Son of the Father, means possessing *partially*, limitedly, what subsists in him as totality and infinitude and in such a way that this participation does not increase or lessen his unity-totality. Behold a gift of God that is analogous — similar and dissimilar — to the gift of being wherein creation is constituted. God Is; He is Being in intensive totality and uniqueness. We *are* only by participation: we have being; we are not Being itself. Hence the multiplicity of creatures does not increase or lessen the uniqueness-totality of the plenitude of Being. As we know by reason and as is confirmed by faith, this reality of creation entails an intimate divine presence in everything, beings are in God: "in him we live and move and have our being" (Acts 17:28). Analogously, to be God's children in a strict but partial sense (to participate in the Word's sonship), is to discover that we are God's children in the Son. Without ceasing to be the Only-begotten, he is first-born among many brethren: "For those whom [God] foreknew he has also predestined to become conformed to the image of his Son, in order that he might be the first-born among many brethren" (Rom 8:29).

As we try to advance in this theological contemplation, we can't forget that "when we approach any of the divine persons, we approach the one God. And when we draw close to all three persons, to the Trinity, again we find ourselves before the one true God."[23] The mystery of being God's children is illuminated even more by the fundamental Christian reality: Christians are to be ever more, not only imitators of Christ, but, in a mysterious but real way, *ipse Christus*: Christ himself.

Being Christ himself

"'I have set my king on Zion, my holy hill. I will tell of the decrees of the Lord: he said to me: "You are my son, today I have begotten you"' (Ps 2:6-7). God our Father in his mercy has given us his Son for king. When he threatens he turns tender; he proclaims his anger, yet gives us his love. 'You are my son': this is addressed to Christ — and to you and me if we decide to become another Christ, Christ himself."[24]

There is only one divine sonship: that of the Word, the Father's Only-begotten. By participating in it we are made God's children: certainly an unfathomable mystery, an unattainable and even incomprehensible goal for our human capacities. But our ever-loving God has given us Christ, the embodied Word, as "the way, the mediator. In him are all things; outside of him there is nothing."[25] All the divine intimacy is revealed to us *in* him, and without him no participation in the sonship is given to us, because Christ, God and man, is that sonship insofar as he is God, and he possesses it fully in virtue of the union *in persona* insofar as he is man.

Christ is the Father's Only-begotten, and we are God's children to the extent we are Christ himself, *ipse Christus*. We will never be able to reach a complete understanding of this reality. Nevertheless, to know that "a Christian is obliged to be *alter Christus, ipse Christus:* another Christ, Christ himself,"[26] as Blessed Josemaria constantly taught, decisively orients our life, our correspondence to the divine action, the only thing capable of making us more and more Christ himself and in him God's children more and more.

"Follow Christ: that's the secret. We must accompany him so closely that we come to live with him as the first twelve did, so closely that we become identified with him. Soon we'll be able to say, provided we have not put obstacles in the way of grace, that we have put on, have clothed ourselves with, Jesus Christ."[27]

The key to intimacy with the Father, Son and Holy Spirit is to follow Christ in such a way that we not only imitate but even identify ourselves with him. Only thus is Jesus the firstborn among many brethren while still the only-begotten Son of the Father. We aren't the Father's children each on his own account; while still ourselves, we are his children because we are Christ.

Through grace and divine filiation, "Christ's life is our life, just as he promised his apostles at the last supper: 'If a man loves me, he will keep my word, and my Father will love him, and we will come to him and make our home with him' (Jn 14:23). That's why a Christian should live as Christ lived, making Christ's sentiments his own, so that he can exclaim with St. Paul: 'It is no longer I who live, but Christ who lives in me' (Gal 2:20)."[28]

To be Christ himself is to have Christ's very sentiments. This speaks to us of our effort to imitate Jesus Christ, not by achieving just an exterior similarity with him, but rather as the result of his living in us as the only-begotten Son, in his unity-distinction with the Father. In this spiritual union whereby we participate in his sonship, we are *in him* children of the Father. All this reality is primarily and essentially a gratuitous gift of God, but requires our cooperation, correspondence: our love, fulfilling his will and commands.

The divine salvific action passes through Jesus' sacred humanity and reaches us from his cross. Perhaps now we can better understand Opus Dei's founder when he shares that light of God: "to have the cross is to be identified with Christ, it is to be Christ and, therefore, to be God's child." To follow our Lord in order to identify ourselves with him is first to seek the cross made present mysteriously but efficaciously by the sacraments, particularly baptism, the Eucharist and penance. "In baptism our Father God takes possession of our lives, makes us share in Christ's life and has given us the Holy Spirit."[29] Above all, the Eucharist, renewing the sacrifice of the cross itself, "gives God's children a divine newness, and we must respond 'by the renewal of your mind' (Rom 12:2), renewing all our feelings and actions. We have been given a new principle of energy, strong new roots grafted onto God."[30]

To be Christian is to be *ipse Christus*, a son or daughter of God. This identification comes to us from the cross' saving power, one then understands how the holy Mass — sacramentally re-presenting the cross — can be "the center and root of a Christian's spiritual life."[31] All our identification with Christ (being God's children) requires embracing Jesus' humanity on the cross. To this encounter is tied another God-given reality: Mary's example, the mediation of Christ's Mother, God's Mother and ours. "To those who draw closer to her and contemplate her life, Mary always does the immense favor of taking them to the cross, of gazing at the example of God's Son. It's at that confrontation where Christian life is decided. And there Mary intercedes, so that our behavior may lead to a reconciliation of the younger brother — you and me — with the firstborn Son of the Father,"[32] reconciliation that becomes identification.

"I have distinguished as it were four stages in our effort to identify ourselves with Christ: seeking him, finding him, getting acquainted with and loving him. It may seem clear that you are only at the first stage. Seek him then, hungrily; seek him within yourselves with all your strength. If you act with determination, I am ready to guarantee that you have already found him and have begun to know and love him and to hold your conversation in heaven (cf. Phil 3:20)."[33]

It is, then, love for Christ, always presupposing faith (Gal 3:26: "you are all sons of God through faith"), that forms Jesus in us, that conforms us to Christ. But it's a love (supernatural charity) that God plants in us; it's participation in Love, in the Holy Spirit. God's charity "is poured forth in our hearts by the Holy Spirit who has been given to us" (Rom 5:5).

In sum: we are God's children in Christ, in the Son, and therefore children of the Father. Nevertheless, the supernatural mystery presents ulterior riches and facets that rightly lead us to contemplate the role of the Holy Spirit in our supernatural adoption. Filiation is *our way* of participating in the infinite fullness of the Trinitarian life; a participation we attain through the sending of the Holy Spirit: Love, the first Gift the Father and the Son send to us.

Through the Holy Spirit

The first fruit, the greatest gift obtained for us through Jesus' cross, resurrection and ascension, is the Holy Spirit. Therefore, "when we participate in the Eucharist," writes St. Cyril of Jerusalem, "we experience the deifying spiritualization of the Holy Spirit, who not only configures us to Christ, as happens in baptism but Christifies us entirely, associating us fully with Jesus Christ."[34]

"This outpouring of the Holy Spirit unites us to Christ and makes us acknowledge that we are God's children. The Paraclete, Love itself, teaches us to saturate our life with the virtue of charity. Thus *consummati in unum*: made one with Christ (cf. Jn 17:23), we can be among all people what the Eucharist is for us, in the words of St. Augustine: 'a sign of unity, a bond of love.'"[35-36]

Made one with Christ by charity (Christified) is to be the Father's children. This charity stems from the outpouring of the Holy Spirit. "The action of the Paraclete within us confirms what Christ had announced: that we are children of God, that we have not received 'the spirit of slavery to fall back into fear, but ... the spirit of sonship. When we cry "Abba! Father!" it is the Spirit himself bearing witness ... that we are children of God' (Rom 8:15-16)."[37]

The Holy Spirit makes us God's children, of the Father in the Son, by Christifying us, by making us *ipse Christus*. It is also the Paraclete who shows us this reality, making us recognize Jesus as Son of God and helping us to recognize ourselves, not as strangers, but as children, when we are identified with him. The Spirit himself reaffirms us in this joyful certainty by means of the gift of piety.[38]

But if we are to affirm that "the Holy Spirit is the Spirit sent by Christ to carry out in us the work of holiness our Lord merited for us on earth,"[39] at the same time we know that every divine action in us (necessarily *ad extra*) is common to the three Divine Persons, to this "one God in three persons: three Divine Persons in the unity of God's substance, in the unity of his love and of his sanctifying action."[40]

Consequently, if we contemplate the mystery from the perspective of efficient causality, we must affirm without any doubt that it is *the whole God* (Father, Son and Holy Spirit) that makes us his children. We can attribute or "appropriate" this action to any of the divine persons, as, for example, the act of creation is attributed to the Father. Concretely, "the sanctification we pray for is attributed to the Paraclete sent to us by the Father and the Son."[41]

Here Blessed Josemaria shows that this appropriation or attribution of the action is precisely the way we express the mysterious reality of the *missions* of the divine persons: we attribute sanctification to the Paraclete, *sent* to us by the Father and the Son. Besides the visible missions of the Son (incarnation) and of the Holy Spirit (Pentecost), grace implies the invisible missions of the Son and the Holy Spirit. These invisible missions are the spiritual creature's real participation — not simply appropriation or attribution — in the eternal processions of the Son and the Holy Spirit.[42] In light of our real deification (our participation in the Son and the Holy Spirit) by the invisible missions, we come to contemplate the deep, supernatural reality of our being *ipse Christus:* therefore, children of the Father through the Holy Spirit.

We can, then, affirm that the Father, Son and Holy Spirit, in the unity of their action *ad extra*, sanctify us, adopt us as God's children. The end of this one divine efficient action is our very godliness, our true introduction into divine life, our union with the Holy Spirit and the Son, sent to our souls as the really distinct persons they are. The Holy Spirit, Love, the common link between the Father and the Son, makes us *ipse Christus*, and in Christ, in the Word, makes us children of the Father. "We have been made children ... of that Father who did not hesitate to give us his dearly beloved Son."[43]

What bright supernatural certainty, knowing that "through Christ and in the Holy Spirit, a Christian has access to the intimacy of God the Father and spends his life looking for the Kingdom which is not of this world, but which is initiated and prepared in this world."[44] Children, then *of* the Father, *through* the Son and *in* the

Holy Spirit; or better, children *of* the Father, *in* the Son, being *ipse Christus, through* the Holy Spirit. The two expressions mean the same thing: human expression cannot do justice to the concepts.

But at the same time, through the unity of the divine action by which we are adopted children of God and by which we become "members of God's family," (Eph 2:19) we can and ought to consider ourselves children of the Trinity: of the Father, Son and Holy Spirit. Thus, for example, Escriva encouraged us to deal with Jesus Christ, our brother, as his own children,[45] because through his humanity he mediates. From his human heart (*perfectus Deus, perfectus homo*) comes the effusion of subsistent Love (the Holy Spirit), who makes us *alter Christus, ipse Christus*. It would be not only irrational but erroneous to eliminate any of the apparently paradoxical aspects by which the profound and illuminating mystery of divine filiation manifests itself in our contemplation.

"It is impossible to speak of these central facts of our faith without feeling the limitations of our minds and the greatness of revelation. Yet even if we cannot fully grasp these truths that overawe our reason, we believe them humbly and firmly. Backed by Christ's testimony, we know they are true. We know that Love in the depths of the Trinity is poured out on all people by the love in Christ's heart."[46]

Children of Mary (and Joseph)

"'A great sign appeared in heaven: a woman with a crown of twelve stars upon her head, adorned with the sun, and the moon at her feet' (Rev 12:1). Mary, virgin without stain, has made up for the fall of Eve: and she has crushed the head of hell's serpent with her immaculate heel. Daughter of God, Mother of God, Spouse of God."[47] It would suffice to consider our Lady's redemptive role and her peerless godliness to learn how to correspond to the divine action inviting us also to be *domestici Dei*: family members with the Father, Son and Holy Spirit.

But Escriva teaches us still more: "Our Lady, holy Mary, will make of you *alter Christus, ipse Christus*: another Christ, Christ himself!"[48] The blessed Virgin obtains the gift of being God's children, because it's only through being *ipse Christus* that we can call God Father. Holy Mary is truly our mother insofar as we are God's children, Christ's brethren. Our divine filiation is at the same time filiation to our Lady. This is because God so willed it: "On Calvary Christ, her most blessed Son and our brother, gave her to us as our Mother, when he said to St. John: 'Behold your Mother' (Jn 19:27),"[49] so that "just as Mary had a major role in the incarnation of the Word, she was intimately involved in the beginning of the Church, Christ's body."[50]

God alone causes our grace and supernatural adoption, but he so arranged things that no grace comes to us except through Mary. From her we receive as mediatrix, in intimate union with her Son, the one mediator, the gift of being God's children; truly from her we are mystically born as his children. To be a child of God is to be *ipse Christus*; to be *ipse Christus* is to be Mary's child. But "it's not enough just to know she is our Mother and as such to think and talk about her. She is your Mother and you her child. She loves you as if you were her only child here on earth. Treat her accordingly: honor and love her; tell her whatever's happening to you. No one will do it for you or as well as you, if you don't do it yourself. I give you my word that, if you set out along this way, you will quickly discover all Christ's love: and you'll find yourself drawn into the ineffable life of God the Father, God the Son and God the Holy Spirit."[51]

Alongside Mary (again because God so willed it) is St. Joseph, since "interior life is nothing but continual and direct conversation with Christ, so as to become one with him. Joseph can tell us many things about Jesus. Therefore, never neglect devotion to him. *Ite ad Ioseph:* Go to Joseph, as Christian tradition puts it in the words of the Old Testament (Gen 41:55)."[52]

By his particular intercession, St. Joseph, who acted as Jesus' father, also acts as father to those eager to identify themselves with Christ. Therefore "St. Joseph really is a father and lord. He protects those who revere him and accompanies them on their journey through this life just as he protected and accompanied Jesus when he was growing up. As you get to know him, you discover that the holy patriarch is also a master of the interior life. He teaches us to know Jesus and share our life with him and to realize that we are part of God's family."[53]

Familiarity with Mary and Joseph leads us to Jesus, to live his life, to identify ourselves with him. And in Jesus — the Father's Only-begotten — we accede to intimacy with the holy Trinity. Escriva called this the path from the "'trinity' on earth to the Trinity in heaven." Thus, "our years on earth, days of work and prayer, will be spent in our Father's presence. If we falter, let's turn to holy Mary, who loves us and teaches us how to pray; and to St. Joseph, our father and lord, whom we venerate so much. On this earth he was the one closest to God's Mother and, after Mary, to her divine Son. Together they'll bring our weakness to Jesus, so he can turn it into strength."[54]

Children of the Church (and of the Pope)

"St. Cyprian has briefly declared: 'it is not possible to have God as Father if you do not have the Church as mother.'"[55-56] In effect, we call it our Mother the Church. "You are holy, O Church, my mother, because the Son of God, who is holy, founded you. You are holy, because the Father, source of all holiness, ordained it. You are holy, because the Holy Spirit, dwelling in the souls of the faithful, assists you in gathering together the Father's children to dwell in the heavenly Church, the eternal Jerusalem."[57]

From this holiness stems the Church's motherhood with respect to all Christians. From and in her we are born to the life of grace through baptism, and our supernatural lives always grow in the Church. Therefore, our birth as God's children is from God but also from the Church. We are God's offspring insofar as we are the Church's children and vice versa: one thing supposes the other. The Church's motherhood in a certain way is an expression or manifestation of God's fatherhood with respect to his adoptive children.

This filiation to the Church has, by divine design, a continuation or manifestation in the necessary filiation of Christians with the Roman Pontiff. "St. Ambrose wrote a few words that comprise, as it were, a song of joy: 'Where Peter is, there is the Church; and where the Church is, not death, but eternal life reigns'[58] For where Peter and the Church are, there is Christ and he is salvation, the only way."[59] We can and ought to say, then, that the Roman Pontiff is truly "father and mother of all Christians."[60]

Brothers and Sisters to All

"Once the redemption had been accomplished, 'there is neither Jew nor Greek; there is neither slave nor freeman' — there is no discrimination of any type — 'for you are all one in Christ Jesus' (Gal 3:28)."[61] The common filiation of many to the one Father necessarily establishes a corresponding brotherhood. If we are God's children, we are brothers and sisters to one another. The reality of this filiation brings with it a real fraternity, which then "is not reduced to a topic of discussion or an illusory ideal."[62]

Being God's children in Christ confers on Christian fraternity some necessary supernatural characteristics. This brotherhood is unity: we are all one in Christ. Brotherhood among Christians shows itself in our being Christ himself, in the reality of the communion of saints, in the mystical body. Ours is not a horizontal but a *vertical relationship in Christ;* it's a stricter, stronger relationship than mere blood ties and incomparably beyond the universal brotherhood of humanity. In some way (mystical but real, with metaphysical content) Christians, more than many brethren, are one: Christ himself.

Similarly, love, the charity the Holy Spirit diffuses in our souls, is what makes us Christ himself, "the distinguishing mark of the apostles and of true Christians in every age is, as we have heard: 'By this all men will know that you are my disciples, if you have love for one another' (Jn 13:35)."[63] The manifestations this fraternity (unity in Christ and love) ought to have in ordinary life are innumerable, but the root from which they grow is always divine filiation. "Be mindful of what others are, and first of all those who are at your side: God's children, with all the dignity that marvelous title entails. We have to behave as God's children toward all God's sons and daughters. Our love is to be a dedicated love, practiced every day and made up of a thousand little details of understanding, hidden sacrifice and unnoticed self-giving. This is the 'fragrance of Christ' that made those who lived among our first brothers in the faith exclaim: 'See how they love one another.'"[64-65]

Behaving as God's children toward all God's children: Opus Dei's founder thus sums up the requirements of fraternal charity made more radical by divine filiation. This supernatural foundation also confers on Christian brotherhood a respect that spells human refinement: love and honor for others, which are love and respect for Christ's image, for Christ himself, in them. Thus we understand the deep supernatural meaning of that counsel: "Feel and live that fraternal spirit, favored child of God, but without familiarities."[66]

Moreover, fraternity extends to everyone, because all are God's creatures and children and called to the intimacy of the Father's home. "All of us are human and all likewise God's children, so we can't think that life consists in building up a brilliant resumé or an outstanding career. Ties of solidarity should bind us all."[67] Indeed, "hunger for justice should lead us to the original source of harmony among mankind: the fact that we are, and know ourselves to be, the Father's children, brothers and sisters."[68]

Despite differences, Christians always ought to be aware that "our Lord has come to bring peace, good news and life to all people. Not only to the rich, nor only to the poor. Not only to the wise nor only to the simple. To everyone, to the brethren, for brothers and sisters we are, children of the same Father God. So there is only one race, the race of God's children. There is only one color, the color of God's children. And there is only one tongue, a language that speaks to the heart and mind, without the noise of words, leading us know God and love one another."[69]

Filial and Fraternal Spirit

Children of God; children of Mary and Joseph; children of the Church and the Roman Pontiff; brothers and sisters to all Christians and all people.... Christian life is to unfold in a climate of filiation and fraternity. Faith should lead us always to feel "at home," however distant from Christ's love are the various settings in which we move.

God's fatherhood, "from whom alll fatherhood in heaven and on earth receives its name" (Eph 3:15), is fostered and manifested by Mary's and the Church's maternal role, and the paternal role played by the Pope and those who can say with St. Paul: "I became your father in Christ Jesus through the Gospel" (1 Cor 4:15). I am moved to think now of Escriva's spiritual paternity to whom can be applied the patriarch's words: "he had other sons and daughters" (Gen 5:4). Christian existence, be it personal or social, grows and develops in one way or another as part of a family. "In your apostolic undertaking don't fear the enemies 'outside,' however great their power. This is the enemy most to be feared: your lack of filial spirit and your lack of fraternal spirit."[70]

Undoubtedly hindrances to harmony and, even more, authentic charity abound. "Peace, truth, unity, justice. How difficult it often seems to eliminate barriers to human harmony! And yet we Christians are called to bring about that miracle of brotherhood. We must work so that everyone with God's grace can live in a Christian way, 'bearing one another's burdens' (Gal 4:2), keeping the commandment of love, which is the bond of perfection and essence of the law (cf. Col 3:14 and Rom 13:19)."[71]

A Child of God Everywhere

Divine filiation is not just another facet of Christian life; in some way it embraces all the others. It is a concrete relationship distinct from sanctifying grace, the virtues, the Paraclete's gifts and so forth. But if we look at the goal of God's plan, we can affirm that all these other helps are given to make us God's children: the supernatural elevation, seen as a whole, is an adoption. Therefore, if being God's children summarizes the new creature, the Christian life consists essentially in comporting ourselves as such. And that means making God's will our own. "What God asks is that you should always act as his children and servants."[72]

Divine filiation is not a particular virtue with acts proper to it. Rather it's a permanent condition of the person, the subject of virtues. One doesn't behave as God's child part of the time. All our activity, the exercise of each virtue, can and ought to ratify our divine filiation. "We are God's children all day long, even though we set aside special moments to consider it. Then we fill ourselves with awareness of our divine filiation, the essence of true piety."[73]

Piety is proper to children. Supernaturally perfected by the corresponding gift of the Holy Spirit, piety aids us to recognize ourselves as God's children and in working consistently at every moment. "Piety born of divine filiation is a profound attitude of the soul that eventually permeates one's entire existence. It is there in every thought, desire, affection."[74] It goes beyond a simple reference to God; it's the certainty of our actual deification, of our living in Christ through the Holy Spirit and thus of our union with the

Father.[75] In consequence, "the whole panorama of our Christian vocation, our unity of life centered on God's fatherly presence, can and ought to be a daily reality."[76]

Though God's children, our actions are entirely our own. By permeating one's whole existence, divine filiation radically stamps all Christian aspects and virtues here on earth, as it will our heavenly citizenship. Again, our faith is the belief of God's children, so too our joy and courage.... It's impossible within our present confines to deal with divine filiation's radical and concrete influence on every aspect of Christian life. What follows concentrates only on those dimensions covering all of Christian existence, direct consequences of our being, and knowing ourselves to be, God's children and brothers and sisters to all people.

The Freedom of God's Children

Human activity is essentially characterized by a freedom that presupposes knowledge. In free actions, our will determines itself (granted of course divine causality sustaining all being). We act, beyond any conditioning, because we so choose. This great natural gift of God to spiritual creatures makes us responsible for our own acts, permitting us to choose and love the good. This freedom of ours is not absolute freedom, something that can never be. From God's free will stem all goods; he creates them. Our duty to orient ourselves toward what is good is independent of our will, and thus arises the possibility of sin, the twisted exercise of freedom. A free creature, until confirmed in grace by definitive union with God, can always abuse freedom. Nevertheless, God in his infinite goodness willed the "risk of our freedom,"[77] since he wants as many of his spiritual creatures as possible to accede to his everlasting intimacy. To know that "God does not want us to be slaves and respects our freedom,"[78] ought to lead us to ask: "What do you want from me, Lord, so that I may freely do it."

"Christ himself gives us the answer: the 'truth will make you free' (Jn 8:32). How great a truth is this, which opens the way to freedom and makes it meaningful throughout our lives. I will sum it up for you, with the joy and certainty that flow from knowing there is a close relationship between God and his creature. It is God-given knowledge that the blessed Trinity looks upon each of us with favoritism, that we are children of so wonderful a Father. I ask my Lord to help us decide to take this truth to heart, to dwell upon it day in and day out; only then will we be acting as free persons. Don't forget: anyone who doesn't realize that he is God's child is unaware of the deepest truth about himself. Absent from his actions are the dominion and self-mastery we find in those who love God above all else."[79]

That God is our Father is the truth setting us free. What is this freedom? It is the freedom proper to human nature, cleansed and elevated by grace, supernatural virtues and gifts of the Holy Spirit. It is ready freedom, supernaturally inclined to goodness, exempt from sin's fetters that make good difficult and supernatural good impossible. The freedom of God's children is fruit of our love for him and his for us. "Freedom finds its true meaning when serving redemptive truth, when spent in seeking God's infinite Love that liberates us from all forms of slavery. Each passing day increases my yearning to proclaim to the four winds the inexhaustible treasure that belongs to Christianity: the glorious freedom of God's children (cf. Rom 8:21)!"[80]

Truth liberates, because it facilitates our choosing and loving the good, which is what freedom is. "Slavery or divine filiation: there's the dilemma we face. Children of God or slaves to pride, to sensuality, to the fretful selfishness afflicting so many souls."[81] There is no such thing as freedom pure and simple, just as there's no such thing as pure nature: there is either nature with grace or nature with sin; there is either the freedom of God's children or interior slavery to one's own wretchedness.

Nevertheless, to fulfill God's will in everything, to choose the good at every juncture, is good bondage: a Christian's condition is also that of serving God. "Either way we'll be slaves. Since we must serve — like it or not, such is our lot — then there is nothing better than recognizing that Love has made us God's slaves. From the moment we recognize this, we cease being slaves and become friends, children. Then we see the difference: we find ourselves tackling honest, secular occupations just as passionately and enthusiastically as others do, but with peace in the depth of our hearts. We are happy and calm, even amid adversity, for we put our trust not in passing things, but in what lasts forever. 'We are not children of the slave but of the free woman' (Gal 4:31).

"Whence our freedom? From Christ our Lord. This is the freedom with which he has ransomed us (cf. Gal 4:31). That's why he teaches, 'if the Son makes you free, you will be free indeed' (Jn 8:36). We Christians need no one to tell us the true meaning of this gift, because the only freedom that can save us is Christian freedom. I like to speak of the adventure of freedom, because that's how your lives and mine unfold. I insist that it is freely, as children and not as slaves, that we follow the path God has marked out for each of us. We relish our freedom of action as a gift from God."[82]

To fulfill God's will, to submit one's mind to the truth and direct freedom toward the good, always toward

God, is not slavery but freedom: a superior freedom united to obedience, to service, to generous dedication. This seems a contradiction, but not so. "Love of God marks out the way of truth, justice and goodness. When we make up our minds to tell God, 'I put my freedom in your hands,' we find ourselves freed from the many chains binding us to trifles, ridiculous worries and petty ambitions."[83]

Since at times it's difficult to behave in accord with this freedom, we go to our Mother: "we can learn to serve with refinement, but without being slavish. In Mary we don't find the slightest trace of the foolish virgins who obey thoughtlessly. Our Lady listens attentively to what God wants, ponders what she doesn't fully understand and asks about what she doesn't know. Then she gives herself completely to doing God's will: 'Behold I am the handmaid of the Lord; let it be to me according to your word' (Lk 1:38). Isn't that marvelous? The blessed Virgin, our teacher in all we do, shows us here that obeying God is not servile, does not bypass our conscience. We should be inwardly moved to discover the 'glorious liberty of God's children' (Rom 8:21)."[84]

Working as God's Children

"I dream, and the dream has come true, of multitudes of God's children, sanctifying themselves as ordinary citizens, sharing the ambitions and endeavors of their colleagues and friends. I want to shout to them about this divine truth: if you find yourselves amid ordinary life, that doesn't mean Christ has forgotten about you or hasn't called you. He has invited you to stay among the world's activities and concerns. He wants you to know that your human vocation, your job and talents, don't fall outside his plans. He has sanctified them and made them a most acceptable offering to his Father."[85]

All God's children, whatever their situation in the world or Church, are called to sanctify themselves, to be each day more Christ himself. They are to see in all circumstances of their ordinary life (work and rest, family and social relations), a reality to be converted into Christ's life: "it is no longer I who live, it is Christ who lives in me" (Gal 2:20).

For too long work has been seen as something demeaning, a punishment, a hindrance to spiritual life. In reality, it is neither punishment, since man has been created "to work" (Gen 2:15), nor does it get in the way of dealing with God. A Christian can and should, with God's grace, "sanctify work, sanctify himself in his work and sanctify others through his work,"[86] a definition of work that extends to every human activity. The reality of divine filiation crowds out slavishness at work, since "in the midst of the limitations accompanying our present life, where sin is still present to some extent at least, we Christians clearly perceive all the wealth of our divine filiation, when we realize that we are fully free because we are doing our Father's work."[87] If we realistically contemplate our life, including the supernatural order, we see there is nothing foreign to the divine plan. Whatever our work, it's our very own, because everything is from God and we are children, not hired hands: "all are yours, and you are Christ's; and Christ is God's" (1 Cor 3:22).

Working with this freedom brings in its wake a generous effort far beyond the search for merely human goals. It all stems from radically knowing oneself to be God's child and knowing likewise the true reward God has promised. "It's good that you serve God as a child, without pay ...

generously. But don't worry if at times you think of the reward."[88] A child of God desires this reward, which is definitive union with Christ and, in him, with the Father and the Holy Spirit. Nevertheless, precisely as a child, "one gladly accepts the need to work in this world and for many years, because Jesus has few friends here below. Let's not turn away from the duty to live our whole life, to the last drop, in the service of God and his Church. And all this, freely: with the freedom of God's children that Jesus won for us by dying on the tree of the cross (cf. Gal 2:20, Rom 8:21)."[89]

This freedom is based on and blended with obedience — in work as in every other aspect of human life — because everything stems from divine filiation. By concentrating on whatever is at hand, a child of God freely seeks to fulfill the Father's will and thus lives with an interior dominion that leads to loving obedience. In every waiting task, one will always discover the will of his Father God himself who comes out to meet him. "Freedom is very close to my heart; that's why I so love the Christian virtue of obedience. We should all realize that we are God's children and should want to fulfill our Father's will. We should do things as God wants them done, *because we feel like it*, which is the most supernatural of reasons."[90] This desire of a good child of God to fulfill the divine will urges a Christian not only to do his own duties as well as possible but also to view others' tasks as one's own or rather God's. "When you have finished your work, do that of your brother, helping him. This, indeed, is virtue befitting a child of God."[91]

So that our work, all our activity, be truly the work of a child of God, it ought to be ever more Christ's work through our identification with him while carrying out all this activity. "While fully involved in his everyday work among others, his equals, busy, under stress, a Christian is to be wholly involved with God, because a child of God."[92] Thus work becomes prayer and apostolate.[93]

The Prayer of God's Children

Through divine filiation, a Christian is to live in God, constantly *divinized*. This is to happen not only passively (because with grace God brings us into his own divine Life) but actively as well (participating with mind and will in the eternal activity of knowing and loving, which is the mystery of the triune God). Our whole life is to be prayer. "In recommending this unbroken union with God, am I not presenting an ideal so sublime that it is unattainable by most Christians? Certainly the goal is high, but not unattainable. The path leading to holiness is a path of prayer; and prayer ought to take root and grow in the soul little by little, like the tiny seed that later develops into a tree with many branches."[94]

To know where this path of prayer begins, the apostles turned to Christ. "We relive the scene where Jesus retired to pray, with his disciples close by, probably contemplating him. When he finished, one decided to ask him: 'Lord, teach us to pray, as John taught his disciples.' And he said to them: 'when you pray, say: Father, hallowed be thy name' (Lk 11:1-2). Note the surprising thing about this reply. The disciples share their daily lives with Jesus, and there, in the course of their ordinary conversations, he tells them how they should pray. He reveals to them the great secret of God's mercy: that we are God's children, who can talk things over with him and spend time with him, just as trustingly as a child does with its father."[95]

Thus does divine filiation characterize Christian prayer, which is nothing if not a child dealing with its

Father. Ours is a dialogue that ordinarily begins with vocal prayers and later continues as contemplation without the noise of words. We trustingly chat with God when we know and feel ourselves to be his own children.[96] With our whole life as its theme, our prayer is bold in petition to God, who is our Father and all-powerful.[97] We air "our joys, sorrows, hopes, annoyances, successes, failures, even the most trivial happenings of the day. We discover that our heavenly Father is interested in everything about us."[98]

With this consoling certainty "in our relationship to God, we are not blind men yearning for light and crying in anguished darkness. We are children who know our Father loves us."[99] Nevertheless, at times, perhaps even habitually, this light is hardly perceived, and the soul finds itself in darkness; seemingly God is far away. Then divine filiation will also be like a powerful root preventing the death of the "trunk" of our prayer, destined to be a fruitful tree.

"I don't mind telling you that at times God has given me many graces. But as a rule I have to go against the grain. I follow my plan, not because I like it, but because I'm required to do so, out of love. 'But, Father,' you ask me, 'can one put on an act for God? Wouldn't that be hypocritical?' Don't worry: for you the time has come to act out a human comedy before a divine spectator. Persevere, for the Father, the Son and the Holy Spirit are contemplating your act; do it all for love of God, to please him, although you find it hard.

"How beautiful to be God's jester! How beautiful to act out such a role for Love, with a spirit of sacrifice, not seeking any personal satisfaction, just to please our Father God who is playing with us! Trustingly turn to God and say to him: 'I don't feel like doing this at all, but I will offer it up for you.' And then put your heart into the job you are doing, even though you think you are just play-acting. Blessed play-acting! I assure you it isn't hypocrisy, because hypocrites need a public for their pantomimes, whereas the spectators of our play, let me repeat, are the Father, the Son and the Holy Spirit, the blessed Virgin, St. Joseph, and all the angels and saints in heaven."[100] This upright Christian attitude in the face of darkness and reluctance extends to work and prayer, to fulfilling any duty. There is no hypocrisy, because we are God's children. If he seems far away, we know that he's playing with us ... at hide and seek!: "rejoicing in his inhabited world" (Prov 8:31).

The sincerity of our prayer amid darkness, as in any other circumstance, is guaranteed if we pray like a child of God; if we're committed to fulfilling our Father's will. "How should we pray? I would go as far as to say, without fear of being mistaken, that there are many, countless, ways of praying. But I would like all of us to pray genuinely, as God's children, not gabbing away like hypocrites who will hear from Jesus' lips: 'Not everyone who says to me, "Lord, Lord!" shall enter the kingdom of heaven' (Mt 7:21). People who live by hypocrisy can perhaps achieve 'the sound of prayer,' says St. Augustine, 'but they cannot possess its voice, because there is no life in them.'[101] They lack the desire to fulfill the Father's will. When we cry 'Lord!' we must do so with an effective desire to put into practice the inspirations the Holy Spirit awakens in our soul."[102]

Nourished by divine filiation, the path of Christian prayer follows, in ever more explicit knowledge and love, the path of our ontological introduction, through adoption in the Son, to the life of the holy Trinity. Our dealings with Christ's most holy humanity, especially on the cross, bring about recognition in him of the Son of God, who opens to us the doors of intra-Trinitarian intimacy. With this prayer not only do we know grace-won intimacy, but we also increase it.

"We started out with the simple and attractive vocal prayers that we learned as children, prayers we ought never to abandon. Our prayer, begun so childlike and ingenuous, now opens out into a broad, smooth-flowing stream, for it follows the course of friendship with him who said: 'I am the Way' (Jn 14:6). If we so love Christ, if with divine daring we take refuge in the lance-opened wound in his side, then the Master's promise will find fulfillment: 'If a man loves me, he will keep my word, and my Father will love him, and we will come to him and make our home with him' (Jn 14:23).

"Our heart now needs to distinguish and adore each of the Divine Persons. The soul is, as it were, making discoveries in the supernatural life, like a little child opening his eyes to the world about him. The soul spends time lovingly with the Father and the Son and the Holy Spirit and readily submits to the work of the life-giving Paraclete, who gives himself to us with no merit on our part, bestowing his gifts and the supernatural virtues!

"'As a deer longs for flowing streams, so longs my soul for thee, O God' (Ps 42:1), thirsting, our lips parched and dry. We want to drink at this source of living water. All day long, without doing anything strange, we move in this abundant, clear spring of fresh waters leaping up to eternal life (cf. Jn 4:14). Words are not needed, because the tongue cannot express itself. The intellect grows calm. One does not reason; one looks! And the soul breaks out once more into song, a new song, because it feels and knows it is under God's loving gaze, all day long.

"I am not talking about extraordinary situations. These are, in all likelihood, ordinary happenings within our soul: a loving craziness which, without any fuss or extravagance, teaches us how to suffer and to live, because God grants us his wisdom. What calm, what peace is ours once we have embarked upon 'the narrow way ... that leads to life' (Mt 7:14).

"Asceticism? Mysticism? I don't care what you call it. What it is doesn't matter. Either way, it's a gift of God's mercy. If you try to meditate, our Lord won't deny you his assistance. Faith and deeds of faith are what matter: deeds, because, as you have known from the beginning and as I told you clearly at the time, God demands more of us each day. This is already contemplation and union. This is the way many Christians should live, each one forging ahead along his own spiritual path (there are countless paths) amid the cares of the world, even though he may not even realize what is happening to him. "Such prayer and behavior don't take us away from our ordinary activities. With our noble human zeal they lead us to God. When men and women offer up all their cares and occupations to God, they make the world divine."[103]

The Apostolate of God's Children

Sanctifying the world, bringing back all things to God, as a consequence of our own divine transformation: this is what Christian apostolate is all about, something based on divine filiation. It necessarily stems from our being Christ himself. In Christ, the one mediator, we are co-redeemers and mediators. "Each one of us is to be *ipse Christus*: Christ himself. He is the one mediator between God and man (cf. 1 Tim 2:5). And we make ourselves one with him to be able to offer all things, with him, to the Father. Our calling to be God's children, in the thick of the world, requires us not only to seek our own personal holiness, but also to go out into all the earth's ways. We'll convert them into roads to lead souls over all obstacles to God. As we take part in all temporal activities, as ordinary citizens, we are to become leaven (cf. Mt 13:33), acting on the dough (cf. 1 Cor 5:6)."[104]

The apostolate of God's children is not one activity among others, neither something added to ordinary life nor superimposed on the constant effort to be identified with Christ. Much less is apostolate a task reserved only to certain Christians. In the same way all of life, work and human realities are to be prayer: Christ's life in us. "For a Christian, apostolate is like breathing. A child of God cannot live without this supernatural life-force."[105]

Since we are Christ himself, we participate in Christ's priesthood, we possess the common priesthood of the faithful, which is one way that Jesus Christ's eternal priesthood (his mediation between God and man) is made present in the world. "Blessed Escriva expounded this doctrine on the common priesthood of the faithful from Opus Dei's very beginning and would always remind the Work's members, lay people professionally dedicated to the most diverse tasks and secular occupations, that, in ways perfectly compatible with *lay mentality*, they also have a *priestly soul*."[106]

Apostolate is not something belonging just to those who participate in Christ's priesthood through the ministerial priesthood (essentially different from the faithful's common priesthood). Winning souls for God is a universal Christian duty. This universality is a direct demand of our identification with Christ, that is, our divine filiation. You cannot separate the vocation to participate personally in the divine intimacy in Christ from the apostolic mission (co-redemption in and with Christ). Analogous to this: "you cannot separate the fact that Christ is God from his role as redeemer. The Word became flesh and came into the world 'to save all men' (1 Tim 2:4). With all our personal defects and limitations, we are other Christs, Christ himself, and we too are called to serve all people."[107]

Any aspect of Christians' apostolic work is extraordinarily illumined by the light of divine filiation. This is the foundation, the root and end, because the apostolic purpose of our life can be summed up as giving "witness to Christ and bringing all those who surround us the joy of knowing that we are God's children,"[108] carrying to all "the new joy that God is a Father who loves without measure."[109]

Christian apostolate is also foreign to any simple tactic of human persuasion (and still less of coercion), since it is a labor of love. It is born of the same supernatural love that the Holy Spirit sends into our souls making us Christ himself, God's children. "A Christian knows that he is grafted onto Christ through baptism. He is empowered to fight for Christ through confirmation, called to act in the world sharing the royal, prophetic and priestly role of Christ. He has become one and the same thing with Christ through the Eucharist, the sacrament of unity and love. And so, like Christ, he has to live for others, loving each and every one around him and indeed all humanity."[110]

True love for others, the only reason for authentic Christian apostolate, is love in Christ. Only in Christ can this apostolate be effective, since only he is redeemer and mediator. "When in Christ's heart we love those who 'are children of the same Father and with us share the same faith and are heirs to the same hope,'[111] then our hearts expand and become fired with a longing to bring everyone closer to God."[112] Only this love permits a child of God "to make up one's mind in Christ to work for the good of souls, without discrimination of any kind; trying to obtain for them, before any other good, the greatest good of all, that of knowing Christ and falling in love with him;"[113] in sum: that all reach the glory of God's children.

To bring all things to God, a Christian, without being anyone's enemy,[114] is nevertheless forced into battle, confronting hardships and occasional retreats, be they real or apparent. In these tough times a child of God, an apostle, always finds the cross, the sign and necessary reality of his identification with Christ. "The cross on your breast? Good. But the cross on your shoulders, the cross in your flesh, the cross in your mind. Thus you will live for Christ, with Christ and in Christ: only thus will you be an apostle."[115]

This cross does not banish joy or optimism from work, from life, which is the means, the sustenance, of apostolate. A Christian ought to know the ineffable truth of these words of Blessed Josemaria : "On the cross you will be Christ, you will feel yourself to be God's child, and you will exclaim: *Abba, Pater!* What joy to meet you, Lord!"

Joy, Sorrow and Death for God's Children

Possessing the good, as well as the hope of enjoying it, brings about a state of soul we call joy. It is an enjoyment rooted either in passing or eternal goods and affecting the soul superficially or profoundly. There are many circumstantial, passing joys. There is laughter that hides sadness and there are tears of joy. "Why do we become dejected? It is because life on earth does not go the way we had hoped, or because obstacles arise that prevent us from satisfying our personal ambitions. Nothing like this happens when a person lives the supernatural reality of his divine filiation. 'If God is for us, who is against us?' (Rom 8:31). As I never tire of repeating: let those be sad who are determined not to recognize that they are God's children!"[116]

There is no fuller joy in this life than that of a child of God, because no good can be compared to the infinite richness of being in God's family, being God's child. Delight, certain hope, serenity, good humor — not "the joy of a healthy animal,"[117] but as the founder also said, "knowing ourselves loved by our Father God, who always seeks us out, helps us and pardons us." This incomparable joy takes root in divine filiation and does not find its support in our own virtues. It is not vain personal satisfaction. In fact, it is built on human frailty and weakness itself. "Don't be afraid to know your real self. That's right, you are made of clay. Don't be worried, for you and I are God's children — and that is the right way of being made divine. We are summoned by a divine call from all eternity: '[The Father] chose us in [Christ] before the foundation of the world, that we should be holy and blameless before him' (Eph 1:4)."[118]

Knowing one's own weakness, experiencing anxiety, doesn't weigh down a child of God, doesn't diminish or stop joy. Indeed such are reasons for joy: "To know we are made of clay ... is a continual source of joy. It means acknowledging our littleness in God's eyes: a little child. Can there be any joy to compare with that of someone, knowing himself to be poor and weak, who knows also that he is God's child?"[119]

Neither can external adversities, obstacles, sorrow, misunderstanding, injustice or betrayal lessen the true joy of God's children. This is not due to lack of realism or superficiality, since "it would be naive to ignore the suffering and discouragement, the sadness and loneliness that meet us relentlessly as we go through life. But our faith has taught us with absolute certainty to see that life's disagreeable side is not due to blind fate, that the creature's destiny is not to rid himself of his desires for happiness. Faith teaches us that everything around and in us is impregnated with divine purpose, that all things echo the call beckoning us to our Father's house.

"This supernatural understanding of earthly existence does not oversimplify the complexity of human life. Rather, it assures us that this complexity can be shot through with God's love, that beyond the disagreeable surface can be discovered the strong and indestructible link binding our life on earth to our definitive life in heaven."[120]

The divine sense of all that happens in our life forms part of our being called to the Father's house. Divine filiation has a precise eschatological dimension: it helps us understand with new lights that the definitive reality of life only comes after death; that today's reality has still not reached its fullness, the fullness of the glory of God's children. Everything in this life, even suffering, tells us that "Christ awaits us. 'Our true homeland is in heaven' (Phil 3:20), while full-fledged citizens of this earth, amid setbacks, injustices and misunderstandings, but also amid the joy and serenity that come from knowing that we are God's children."[121] "This supernatural admission of sorrow simultaneously acknowledges the greatest victory. Jesus, dying on the cross, has conquered death; God draws life from death. The attitude of God's child is not one of resignation to a tragic failure. It is the satisfaction of one who has tasted victory."[122]

Moreover, sorrow can be the root of increasing joy, because for a Christian to find suffering is to find the cross and thereon he or she is *ipse Christus*, a child of God. So, "if we obey God's will, the cross will mean our own resurrection and exaltation. Christ's life will be fulfilled step by step in our own lives. It will be said of us that we have tried to be God's good children, who went about doing good in spite of our weakness and personal shortcomings, however many."[123]

In this, as in everything else, the teaching of Opus Dei's founder followed the actual experience of his life, a life God wanted to mark profoundly with the sign of the cross. Even in the hardest situations "the Father always kept his good humor. Those of us at his side in those moments never saw him sad. On the contrary, he was always joyful and optimistic. The source of that serenity was a deep awareness of divine filiation — something God wanted as the very foundation of Opus Dei's spirit."[124]

And death? That decisive moment can neither terrify God's child nor cloud his luminous joy, because "for God's children, death is life"[125] — the final bound to fulfillment. And God's judgment? It serves as a goad to constant conversion, to rectifying one's intention. To God's child is addressed this simple but poignant question: "Does your soul not burn with the desire to make your Father God happy when he has to judge you?"[126] "Without fear of life and without fear of death." Who can affirm this, as Blessed Josemaria did before thousands of people, but a child of God?

"Thus, almost without realizing it, we go forward at God's pace, taking strong and vigorous strides. We'll come to sense deep in our hearts that, when close to God, we can find joy in suffering, self-denial and sorrow. What a great source of strength for God's child to know himself so close to his Father! That's why, my Lord and Father, no matter what happens, I stand firm and secure with you, because you are my rock and my strength (cf. 2 Kng 22:2)."[127]

The Conversion of God's Children

Christian life on earth, beginning with baptism and ending with passage to true Life, is not a steadily ascending path. "We'd be mistaken if we thought that our longing to seek Christ, our meeting and getting to know him and enjoying the sweetness of his love, makes us immune from sin."[128] We well know we're sinners so long as life lasts. Therefore "we should not be surprised to find, in our body and soul, the needle of pride, sensuality, envy, laziness and desires to dominate others. Those all form the point of departure, the usual context for winning in this intimate sport, this race toward our Father's house."[129]

Our weakness is the context where we approach God. This can only be understood in the light of divine mercy, knowing that "God in taking care of us as a loving father looks on us 'in his mercy' (Ps 25: 6), a mercy that is 'tender' (Ps 108: 21), welcome as 'clouds of rain' (Sir 35:20)."[130] Surrounded by personal weakness and sin, our Father God's mercy moves us and constantly attracts us toward himself. With all our sins and weaknesses we go to the Father and we *return* to him; we are converted.

Conversion and penance aren't realities only touching a Christian now and then. Ours is to be a permanent conversion, one illumined, characterized in its essence, by a divine filiation that constantly confirms us in a consoling truth: "men do not scandalize God. He can put up with all our infidelities. Our heavenly Father pardons any offense when his child returns to him, when he repents and asks for pardon. The Lord is such a good Father that he anticipates our desire to be pardoned and comes forward to us, opening his arms laden with grace.

"Now I'm not inventing anything. Remember the parable Jesus told to help us understand the love of our heavenly Father, the one about the prodigal son? 'But while he was yet at a distance, his father saw him and had compassion, and ran and embraced him and kissed him' (Lk 15:20). That's what the sacred text says: he covered him with kisses. Can you describe more graphically God's paternal love for men?

"When God runs toward us, we cannot keep silent; rather with St. Paul we exclaim: *Abba Pater!*: Father, my Father! (Rom 8:15). Though the creator of the universe, he doesn't mind our not using high-sounding titles, nor worry about our not acknowledging his greatness. He wants us to call him Father; he wants us to savor that word, our souls filling with joy."[131] Here also Escriva's word and example guide us, since "truly, love and humility were two constants in the holy life of our Father, who infused a filial daring into his prayer and apostolic activity. The upshot was a continual beginning and beginning again in interior life. His life traced the prodigal son's path, always returning with wholehearted trust to the mercy of God his Father."[132] We are always to play the prodigal son and not just when we have sinned gravely. We are to begin again each day with a steady spirit of penance that robs no joy from our day, because ours is a joyful conversion, that of God's children.

Often we forget these realities, and so we must reserve some time of the year to intensify and renew our desires and works of conversion. "At times the Lenten liturgy, with its emphasis on the consequences of man's abandonment of God, has a suggestion of tragedy, but there is more to it. It is God who has the last word, and it's the word of his saving and merciful love and, therefore, the word of divine filiation."[133]

Through pride alone we can frustrate the divine and human marvel of a joyful conversion. Pride either precludes acknowledgment of our own sin or leads us to believe there's no remedy for it. So a good child of God is humble, struggles to be so. This humility has nothing to do with diffidence. It is founded on divine filiation and leads to confident prayer. "When faced with weaknesses and sins, with our mistakes (even though, by God's grace, they be of little account), let's turn to God our Father in prayer and say to him, 'Lord, here I am in my wretchedness and frailty, a broken vessel of clay. Bind me together again, Lord, and then, helped by my sorrow and your forgiveness, I shall be stronger and more attractive than before!' What a consoling prayer, which we can say every time something fractures the miserable clay of which we're made.

"Let's not be surprised at our frailty. Let it not come as a shock to see how easily our good behavior breaks down, for little or no reason. Trust in God, whose help is always at hand. 'The Lord is my light and my salvation; whom shall I fear?' (Ps 27:1). No one. If we thus approach our heavenly Father, we'll have no grounds for fearing anyone or anything."[134]

How striking to hear Escriva affirm: "I fear nothing and no one; not even God who is my Father!" We ought to claim this too because, knowing ourselves God's children through the gift of piety granted by the Holy Spirit, we are assured of the gift of fear of the Lord in its fullest supernatural sense. "The fear of the Lord is holy. This fear is a son's veneration for his Father — never a servile fear. For God, your Father, is not a tyrant."[135] When we've lacked this veneration, when we've abused God's love, "awareness that God is our Father brings joy to our conversion: it tells us that we are returning to our Father's house."[136]

Conclusion: the Father's Little Children

"As newborn babes ... *quasi modo geniti infantes* (1 Pet 2:2). It occurred to me that the Church's invitation today is very well suited to all of us who feel the reality of our divine filiation. It is certainly right that we be very strong, very solid persons of mettle who can influence our environment; yet, before God, how good it is to see ourselves as little children!"[137]

When we stop to consider who God is, however slight the extent we can do so, it becomes apparent we are little children being led along paths of spiritual infancy. So we should try to live as children, avoiding the folly of acting grown-up. Yes, there is a definite maturity for God's children, but it consists in full identification with Jesus Christ, "the fullness of Christ" (Eph 4:13), which we will only reach in heaven if we are faithful.

We are destined to this incomparable grandeur, and in order to reach it Jesus Christ himself has shown us the indispensable condition of *becoming children* (cf. Mt 18:3). But "to be little you have to believe as children believe, to love as children love, to abandon yourself as children do ... to pray as children pray."[138] There are thousands of ways to live this spiritual childhood, but in each case living as God's little children "is not spiritual foolishness or softness; it is a sane and forceful way which, due to its difficult easiness, the soul must begin and then continue, led by the hand of God."[139]

To put all our trust in God, we need to feel ourselves small children of God all-powerful. In a very special way, this attitude is fundamental for conversion to last. "In our interior life, it does all of us good to be *quasi modo geniti infantes*, like those tiny tots who seem to be made of rubber and even enjoy falling down. They get up again right away and are once more running around, for they know their parents will always be there to console them, whenever needed."[140]

"If we try to act like them, our stumbles and failures in the interior life (which, moreover, are inevitable) will never result in bitterness. Our reaction will be one of sorrow but not of discouragement, and we'll smile with a smile that gushes up like fresh water from the joyous awareness that we are children of that love, of the grandeur, the infinite wisdom, the mercy, that is our Father.

"We have to learn how to be God's children. Meanwhile, we're to pass on to others this outlook, which, however many our natural weaknesses, will make us 'strong in the faith' (1 Pet 5:9), fruitful in good works and certain of our way. Then, no matter what kind of mistakes, even the most embarrassing, we'll never hesitate to react and return to the sure path of divine filiation, which ends up in the open and welcoming arms of our Father God."[141]

Divine filiation is our goal and brings us to true fullness, to the glory of God's children. Living so, as children of the Father, "I end with our Lord's words of greeting, *Pax vobis!* Peace be with you ... 'Then the disciples were glad when they saw the Lord' (Jn 20:19-20), this Lord who accompanies us to the Father."[142]

Having reached the end of this survey of Escriva's teachings on divine filiation, I am sure that I have not known how to express the full theological richness contained in his words. This in itself serves to highlight the exceptional heights of contemplation he reached and his not inconsiderable contribution to theological science and to theological *life*.

On the other hand, the direct reading of the texts that weave these pages together will make even clearer the capital importance of the unitary vision of Christian existence rooted in divine filiation. This was effectively demonstrated in the life of Blessed Escriva in all its ineffable depth: as the direct connection of the supernatural order with the divine life of the holy Trinity; as identification with Christ; as root of authentic freedom; as the foundation for all Christian life, even its most ordinary aspects.

This supernatural radicalism gives a profound sense to all the other great themes — sanctifying one's work, family and social life, and so forth — where Escriva has made theological contributions. These pages are also a testimony of filial thanksgiving to one who has not only been a master of theological understanding of the highest mysteries, but also a Father who has cleared this great path God has given us: recognizing our divine filiation.

Notes

[1] A. del Portillo, Foreword, *Christ is Passing by*. [All the following citations where no author is mentioned are Escriva's works.]
[2] *The Way*, no. 274.
[3] *Friends of God*, no. 143.
[4] A. del Portillo, *op. cit.*
[5] *Christ is Passing by*, no. 65.
[6] A. del Portillo, "Monseñor Escriva de Balaguer, instrumento de Dios," *En memoria de Mons. Josemaria Escriva de Balaguer*, Pamplona 1976, p. 45.
[7] Text of the prayer to Blessed Josemaria .
[8] Quoted by A. del Portillo, "Mons. Escriva de Balaguer, testigo del amor a la Iglesia," *Palabra*, June 1976, p. 9.
[9] *Christ is Passing by*, no. 64.
[10] *Conversations with Monsignor Escriva*, no. 64.
[11] *Christ is Passing by*, no. 100.
[12] Ibid., no. 133.
[13] Ibid., no. 65.
[14] Cf. Ibid., no. 64.

[15] Ibid., no. 21.
[16] Ibid., no. 48.
[17] Ibid., no. 103.
[18] Ibid., no. 133.
[19] Ibid., no. 160.
[20] *Conversations*, no. 67.
[21] *Friends of God*, no. 252.
[22] *Christ is Passing by*, no. 66.
[23] Ibid., no. 91.
[24] Ibid., no. 185.
[25] Ibid., no. 91.
[26] Ibid., no. 96. Cf. *Conversations*, no. 58.
[27] *Friends of God*, no. 299.
[28] *Christ is Passing by*, no. 103.
[29] Ibid., no. 128.
[30] Ibid., no. 155.
[31] Ibid., no. 87.
[32] Ibid., no. 149.
[33] *Friends of God*, no. 300.
[34] *Catechesis*, 22, 3.
[35] *In Ioannis Evangelium tractatus*, 26, 13: PL 35, 1613.
[36] *Christ is Passing by*, no. 87.
[37] Ibid., no. 118.
[38] Cf. *Friends of God*, no. 92.
[39] *Christ is Passing by*, no. 130.
[40] Ibid., no. 86.
[41] Ibid., no. 85.
[42] Cf. St. Thomas Aquinas, *Summa Theologiae*, I, q. 43.
[43] *Friends of God*, no. 228.
[44] *Christ is Passing by*, no. 116.
[45] Cf. Ibid., no. 165.
[46] Ibid., no. 169.
[47] *Holy Rosary*, fifth glorious mystery.
[48] *Christ is Passing by*, no. 11.
[49] Ibid., no. 171.
[50] Ibid., no. 141.
[51] *Friends of God*, no. 293.
[52] *Christ is Passing by*, no. 56.
[53] Ibid., no. 39; cf. *The Way*, no. 559.
[54] *Friends of God*, no. 255.
[55] *De catholicae Ecclesiae unitate*, 6; PL 4, 502.
[56] *In Love with the Church*, no. 29.
[57] Ibid., no. 8.
[58] *In XII Ps. Enarratio*, 40, 30.

[59] *In Love with the Church*, no. 11.
[60] Ibid., no. 13.
[61] *Christ is Passing by*, no. 38.
[62] *Friends of God*, no. 236.
[63] Ibid., no. 224.
[64] Tertullian, *Apologeticum*, 39: PL 1, 471.
[65] *Christ is Passing by*, no. 36.
[66] *The Way*, no. 948.
[67] *Friends of God*, no. 76.
[68] *Christ is Passing by*, no. 157.
[69] Ibid., no. 106.
[70] *The Way*, no. 955.
[71] *Christ is Passing by*, no. 157.
[72] Ibid., 60.
[73] *Conversations*, no. 102.
[74] *Friends of God*, no. 146.
[75] Cf. *The Way*, no. 267.
[76] *Christ is Passing by*, no. 11.
[77] Ibid., 113.
[78] Ibid., no. 129.
[79] *Friends of God*, no. 26.
[80] Ibid., no. 27.
[81] Ibid., no. 38.
[82] Ibid., no. 35.
[83] Ibid., no. 38.
[84] *Christ is Passing by*, no. 173.
[85] Ibid., no. 20.
[86] Ibid., no. 45.
[87] Ibid., no. 138.
[88] *The Way*, no. 669.
[89] *Friends of God*, no. 297.
[90] *Christ is Passing by*, no. 17.
[91] *The Way*, no. 440.
[92] *Christ is Passing by*, no. 65.
[93] Cf. Ibid., no. 49.
[94] *Friends of God*, no. 295.
[95] Ibid., no. 145; cf. *Conversations*, no. 102.
[96] Cf. *Christ is Passing by*, no. 64.
[97] Cf. *The Way*, nos. 892, 893, 896.
[98] *Friends of God*, no. 245.
[99] *Christ is Passing by*, no. 142.
[100] *Friends of God*, no. 152.
[101] *Enarrationes in Psalmos*, 139, 10; PL 37, 1809.
[102] *Friends of God*, no. 243.

[103] Ibid., nos. 306-308.
[104] *Christ is Passing by*, no. 120; cf. no. 183.
[105] Ibid., no. 122; cf. *The Way*, no. 919.
[106] A. del Portillo, "Mons. Escriva...," *Palabra*, p. 6.
[107] *Christ is Passing by*, no. 106.
[108] Ibid., no. 30.
[109] Ibid., no. 100.
[110] Ibid., no. 106; cf. *Conversations*, no. 1.
[111] Minucius Felix, *Octavius*, 31; PL 3, 338.
[112] *Friends of God*, no. 226.
[113] Ibid., no. 231.
[114] Cf. *Christ is Passing by*, no. 124.
[115] *The Way*, no. 929.
[116] *Friends of God*, no. 108.
[117] *The Way*, no. 659.
[118] *Christ is Passing by*, no. 160.
[119] *Friends of God*, no. 108.
[120] *Christ is Passing by*, no. 177.
[121] Ibid., no. 126; cf. *The Way*, nos. 692, 864.
[122] *Christ is Passing by*, no. 168.
[123] Ibid., no. 21.
[124] A. del Portillo, "Mons. Escriva...," *En Memoria...*, p. 39.
[125] *Friends of God*, no. 79.
[126] *The Way*, no. 746.
[127] *Friends of God*, no. 246.
[128] Ibid., no. 303.
[129] *Christ is Passing by*, no. 75.
[130] Ibid., no. 7.
[131] Ibid., no. 64.
[132] A. del Portillo, "Mons. Escriva..." *En Memoria...*, p. 22.
[133] *Christ is Passing by*, no. 66.
[134] *Friends of God*, no. 95.
[135] *The Way*, no. 435.
[136] *Christ is Passing by*, no. 64.
[137] *Friends of God*, no. 142.
[138] *Holy Rosary*, preface.
[139] *The Way*, no. 855; cf. no. 853; *Christ is Passing by*, no. 10.
[140] *Friends of God*, no. 146; cf. *The Way*, no. 887.
[141] *Friends of God.*, no. 146.
[142] Ibid., no. 149.